OM Publishing
CARLISLE, UK.

Corrie ten

Faith in dark places

Dedication: For John

Sue Shaw

ISBN 1-85078-102-8

British Library Cataloguing in Publication
Data

Shaw, Sue
    Corrie ten Boom : Faith in Dark Places
    I. Title   II. Salisbury, Martin
    269.2092

    ISBN 1–85078–102–8

OM Publishing is an imprint of STL Ltd,
PO Box 300, Carlisle,
Cumbria CA3 0QS, UK

Designed and created by
Three's Company,
12 Flitcroft Street,
London WC2H 8DJ

Author: Sue Shaw
Illustrations by Martin Salisbury

Worldwide co-edition organised and
produced by Angus Hudson Ltd,
Concorde House,
Grenville Place,
London NW7 3SA

Printed in Singapore.

San Quentin prison, California. One Sunday morning, a silver-haired old lady walked into the prison chapel. She looked around at the many harsh, haggard faces. These were some of the most violent and dangerous criminals in America. What could an old woman have to say that would interest such men? What was she doing in a prison anyway?

She began, 'When we know Jesus, we can have real joy. He is always with us. When we do wrong, he gives us the strength to be good. When we are afraid, he helps us to love.'

As she spoke, faces began to change. Some of the men smiled. They were listening hard. At the end of her talk, the men jumped up to applaud and cheer. This had never happened before at San Quentin. Who was this woman?

She was Corrie ten Boom, a Dutch woman; and she too had once been a prisoner. Her crime had been to rescue Jewish people from German soldiers during the Second World War. Her punishment had been hard labour in a German prison camp.

Corrie knew how violent and cruel people can be, and that prison life can be harsh. Yet she trusted in a loving God. He had been with her in prison, and she wanted people to know that this could be true for them too.

No-one returns alive!
During the Second World War Corrie had been jailed in Ravensbruck, a place far worse than any American prison. It was one of many prison camps used by the Germans to imprison millions of people during the war, and it was known as the camp from which no-one returned alive. In Ravensbruck, thousands of innocent people died of hunger or disease. Thousands more were shot or gassed. Starving women were cruelly crammed into filthy, cold buildings by well-fed and well-clothed guards.

How unlike Corrie's home in the city of Haarlem in Holland There she had enjoyed fun and laughter, food and warmth, beauty and peace. Every mealtime the ten Boom family sat round the oval dining table, where there was always hot, nourishing food, even when money was short. They had parties games and songs round the piano, and visitors were always made welcome.

Corrie's home was a tall, narrow house with steep, winding stairs. In fact, it was two houses. The one in front was three floors high, with two rooms on each level. The back wall had been knocked down to join it to a narrower house at the back. With all these rooms, it was possible to hide many Jews during the war.

Corrie, the youngest of four children, lived here with her parents, two sisters, a brother and three aunts. When Corrie was born, in the winter of 1892, she was blue with cold. She cried and cried.

Since there were no incubators for weak babies in those days, her Auntie Anna rolled Corrie in her apron and tied her against her stomach, where she kept warm and quiet.

'Mischief was my middle name!'

Corrie soon grew into a lively and adventurous girl. 'I was no angel,' she wrote. 'Mischief was my middle name. I did everything with my best friend, cousin Dot. We played tag, went skating when the canals were frozen over. But our favourite game was hide-and-seek in the old cathedral. There were so many wonderful places to hide.' Corrie was never scared of the huge building, even in the dark. She knew that God was watching over her.

Corrie's parents trusted God in good and bad times. Father ten Boom read to his family from the Bible every day, and helped the children learn verses off by heart. He also wanted them to understand other languages, so he collected many Bibles written in different languages. Whenever one of the children read out a Bible verse in Dutch, another child read the same verse in another language. In this way they all learned a little German, French, English, Greek and Hebrew.

As Corrie grew up, she knew more and more Bible verses in other languages. This turned out to be very helpful when she was in prison with women from other countries.

Watchmaking

Corrie's father was an expert watchmaker. With great patience he lovingly repaired watches and clocks sent to him from all over Holland. When Corrie was growing up, she asked if she could be a watchmaker too. 'Then you must have the best education,' her father said.

Corrie was sent to work in a watch factory in Switzerland. It was very unusual in those days for a woman to travel away from home on business. After a few months she returned home and her father taught her all that he knew. Corrie became the first licensed woman watchmaker in the whole of Holland.

While Corrie and her father worked in the shop, her elder sister, Betsie, took care of the cleaning and cooking. After Corrie's mother and aunts died, the house seemed very empty.

But it wasn't long before the house was filled with the sound

of children. After the First World War, thousands of German boys and girls lost their homes and families. The ten Boom family fostered many of these children until they were old enough to go back to Germany. Many children of missionaries also came to stay, while their parents were working overseas.

Corrie spent her evenings running Christian clubs for teenagers. On Sundays she taught mentally-handicapped children about God and his love for them. Corrie knew that God cared for every person, whether they were clever or not.

Her brother, Willem, also cared for others. With his wife, Tine, he ran a nursing home for elderly Jewish people. Long before it happened, Willem sensed that Jews would be treated cruelly, so he wanted to do all he could to show them love.

The years sped by. Corrie and Betsie, neither of whom married, were busy and active. Father ten Boom, although over eighty years old, still worked at his bench in the shop.

War!

In 1939 their peace was broken by the news of war. Germany invaded Poland, then Belgium. Holland tried not to take sides, but it made no difference. Hitler's troops attacked.

One night Corrie and Betsie heard the bombs dropping on nearby Schiphol airport. Corrie ran to Betsie's room. They sat with their arms round each other and prayed, 'Lord make us strong. Take away our fear. Help us to trust.'

The bombing continued for five more days. The small Dutch army was overpowered by the larger German forces.

At first little changed in Haarlem. But slowly the Germans began to give orders. No-one could leave their house after six o'clock in the evening. Ration cards were issued for food. Soldiers took away Dutch people's bikes, cars, tin, gold and radios.

The Germans passed a law forbidding any Jews to work in government offices, schools or universities. Another law forced everyone over the age of fifteen to carry an identity card. Jews had the letter 'J' stamped on their cards.

'No Jews!'
Signs were put up throughout the city. In shop windows they read: 'JEWS WILL NOT BE SERVED'. In restaurants, parks, libraries and concert halls the signs announced 'NO JEWS'. People mysteriously disappeared. Houses suddenly became empty.

Night after night British and German planes fought overhead. One night Corrie tossed and turned. It was impossible to sleep. She heard her sister making tea downstairs in the kitchen, so she slipped out of bed to join her. They chatted until the skies were quiet.

When Corrie finally climbed back into bed in the dark, she touched something hard and sharp. She felt blood trickling down her fingers. *What's this?* she thought. On her pillow lay a twenty-five centimetre long piece of metal. It was a fragment of exploded bomb! Corrie realised that if she hadn't gone downstairs, she would have been killed.

One day, when Corrie and her father went for their usual walk along the narrow, cobble-stoned streets, they were surprised to see people they knew wearing a yellow star on their coats. The word *Jood* (Dutch for 'Jew') was written in the centre.

Father ten Boom turned to his daughter. 'Corrie, will you buy a yellow star for me? These are my friends. I will wear one as well.'

'No, Father,' said Corrie. 'You might disappear too!'

A hiding place
Hitler and his followers wanted to destroy all Jews in Europe. Corrie and her family began to see friends and neighbours being attacked. Four German soldiers forced their way into the fur shop across the street. The shop owner, Mr Weil, stood in the street, helpless, as the soldiers came out, their arms loaded with coats.

Corrie ran out to Mr Weil. 'Quick!' she said, 'You must come inside.'

Clearly it was too dangerous for Mr Weil to stay in his shop. Father, Corrie and Betsie all agreed it would be safer for him to stay with brother Willem in the country. That night Willem's son, Kik, came to fetch him.

Soon news spread that the ten Boom family could be trusted to help Jews. After Mr Weil came women, teenagers and old couples, all frightened of being arrested. With help, Corrie found safe homes for them all over Holland and elsewhere in Europe.

Corrie's bedroom became an office and a hiding place. A false brick wall was built across her room, with a small sliding door in one corner. This created a tiny hidden room, with just enough space for eight people to squeeze in. On the floor was a mattress, a jug of water, vitamin tablets and dry biscuits.

'The Germans could search for a year', said the man who designed it, proudly. 'They'll never find this one!'

Soon there were six people living secretly in the house. Eussie, Mary and Thea were all Jews; Peter, Hans and Leendert were Dutchmen who refused to work for the Germans.

Workmen fixed electric buzzers in every room, in case of a surprise attack by German soldiers. As soon as the buzzer was pressed, those who had to hide raced up to the secret room. The others made the house look as if only three people lived there. On their first practice this all took four long minutes, but after many rehearsals they brought the time down to seventy seconds.

Spy!

One morning a stranger came to the door. 'My wife has been arrested,' he said. 'She has been helping many Jews. There's a policeman who will set her free if I can find 600 guilders. Will you help us?' Corrie agreed.

But the man was a spy. No sooner had he taken the money than he reported to the Germans that Corrie was helping the Jews.

Corrie, who had gone back to bed suffering with flu, was

suddenly wakened by the alarm. Six people raced across her room and dived through the panel. Seconds later a stranger burst through the door.

'Where is your secret room?' he demanded.

'I don't know what you're talking about.'

'Never mind. We'll have the house watched until they're turned into mummies,' he growled.

He ordered Corrie downstairs. The house was ransacked and valuables seized. A total of thirty-five people was arrested that day. Armed guards took to the police station all of father ten Boom's children, a grandson, and many visitors to the house.

Next day, at the Nazi headquarters, they were each questioned. The chief interrogator looked at father ten Boom. 'I'd like to send you home, old fellow,' he said. 'Just give me your word that you won't cause any more trouble.'

'If I go home today,' father replied, 'I will open my door to anyone in need who knocks.'

After that he was treated the same as the others. The questioning went on for many more hours, then they were transferred to a larger prison some miles away.

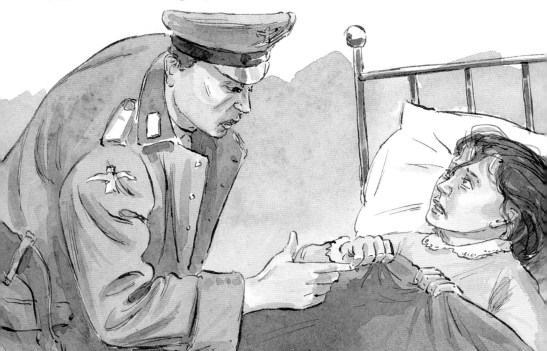

Separated

'Women prisoners, follow me!' shrieked a woman guard.

'Father,' Corrie cried, 'God be with you!'

'And with you, my daughters,' he said.

The doors clanged shut. *Oh father, when will I see you again?* thought Corrie.

Corrie was put in a small, filthy cell with five other women. Her flu worsened and developed into pleurisy, a serious chest disease. To stop the disease spreading to other prisoners, she was moved to a cell on her own.

A kind nurse slipped four Gospels into Corrie's pocket. For seven long weeks Corrie sat alone, reading, praying and hoping.

A parcel arrived containing a sweater, towel, biscuits, vitamins, needles and thread. Underneath the stamp she read a secret message: 'All the watches in your cupboard are safe.' Corrie was thrilled. 'Watches' was the code word for Jews. The hiding place had not been discovered after all!

More lonely days passed. Then Corrie received her first letter from home.

'Corrie, can you be very brave?' it began. 'Father lived only ten days after his arrest. He is now with Jesus . . .' Corrie was deeply upset, but she knew that she would see her father again in heaven.

A few days later a German officer came to her cell.

'Come to my office. The lawyer has come.'

'Lawyer?' Corrie asked.

'For the reading of your father's will.'

Riches!

Suddenly Corrie found herself back with her family: her sisters Betsie and Nollie, Nollie's husband Flip, her brother Willem and his wife Tine. The officer kindly turned away and allowed them to talk. Nollie silently pressed a small package into Corrie's hand. It was a Bible tucked inside a bag with a drawstring. Corrie slipped the string over her head, so that the bag was hidden down her back. She felt so rich!

The will was read and Willem prayed for them all, including the officer. Seconds later they were back in their cells. But they had been together!

Shortly afterwards Nollie, Flip, Tine and Willem were released. Only Corrie and Betsie remained prisoners.

By early June 1944, Corrie had been alone in her cell for four months. One morning she was startled to hear the guards yelling.

'Get your things together! Prepare to evacuate.' What was happening? Had the Germans been defeated?

Hours later all the prisoners were herded into vans and driven to a nearby railway station. Corrie spotted Betsie among the crowd. She pushed and nudged her way through, until she could grab Betsie's hand.

Prison camp

It was so good to be together. Squashed into a slow-moving, unlit train, they talked and talked. Hours later the train stopped. Guards screamed, 'Get out! Get out!' They stumbled

onto the tracks and began a long march in the dark. At last they reached Vught, a prison camp in the south of Holland.

Life at the camp soon became a dull routine. Everyone was made to work for eleven hours each day. Corrie helped put together radio parts, while Betsie, who was weaker, worked in the sewing room. In the evenings they held secret prayer meetings round their bunk. Women crowded together to hear words from the Bible.

The nights were often short, because they were ordered out of bed for roll-call at three or four o'clock in the morning.

A barbed-wire fence separated the women from the men's camp. One day they heard the sound of guns firing over and over again. More than 180 men prisoners died that day.

Husbands, brothers and sons had been killed within their hearing. Soon Corrie and Betsie were surrounded by heart-broken women who needed someone to listen and to care. Many more women joined in their prayer times. Many more found real hope in God's promise of life after death for those who love and trust Jesus.

As the weeks passed, the sound of the firing squad was heard more often. One day the shooting lasted two hours. Another 700 prisoners had died.

How much longer can we bear this? thought Corrie.

Ravensbruck
The very next day, all prisoners were ordered to be moved to camps in Germany. Guards pushed them into empty cargo trains, jabbing with their guns. For the next four days and nights the train crawled along, deeper and deeper into Germany. Cramped together, the women fought over crusts of dry bread and sips of water. At last the train stopped and the doors opened. The hungry, exhausted women stumbled out. Sunlight! Fresh air!

'March!' came the order. They staggered along country lanes, too weak to run away.

At the top of a small hill they looked down on a vast, grey

concrete building - Ravensbruck! Every heart trembled at the name. This was the terrible women's camp, where hundreds were killed every day.

Corrie felt the little Bible bumping on her back. *As long as I have God's word, I can face even this,* she thought.

In the middle of the night they were ordered to form a queue outside the shower rooms. Ahead of the two sisters women were taking off their clothes, leaving them in a great heap.

'Our Bible. How can we keep it without being found out? God, help us,' Corrie prayed. 'Where are the toilets?' she asked a guard.

Jerking his head towards the shower room he snarled, 'Use the drains!'

Betsie and Corrie walked into the empty room. In a few minutes it would be full of naked, shivering women. In a flash, Corrie whipped off the Bible bag and, along with some warm underwear and a medicine bottle, she tucked it behind some rotting, slimy benches.

Ten minutes later the two sisters were under the icy-cold showers. On the floor lay a pile of thin cotton dresses. Corrie and Betsie pulled theirs on. Corrie reached behind the bench for the precious bundle and stuffed it inside her dress. It was impossible to hide the bulge.

Protected
'Please God,' Corrie prayed, 'send your angels to surround me.'

As they trooped out of the shower room, the guards ran their hands over each prisoner. The woman in front of Corrie was searched three times. No-one touched Corrie!

Seeing that everyone was to be searched again by women guards, Corrie slowed down. The woman in charge pushed Corrie roughly past the search point. 'Move along! You're holding up the line,' she snapped.

So, when Corrie and Betsie reached their barrack room, they still had their Bible. What a wonderful answer to prayer!

Between five and seven women had to share each single

bunk. They slept sideways on bedding that was full of fleas and dust. At four-thirty each morning they had to turn out for roll-call. At first it only lasted an hour, but later it sometimes stretched to several hours. In the cold weather, some women sank to their knees, too weak to stand any longer.

Every week the women prisoners were forced to stand naked in front of male guards, as they were examined by three doctors. One looked at their teeth, another at their throats, another between their fingers. Being naked was just to make them feel worthless.

Corrie remembered how Jesus had hung naked on a cross. 'Thank you, Jesus. You understand how this feels,' she prayed. 'You suffered for me. Give me strength and help me to bear this.'

Whenever the women prisoners were left alone, Corrie and Betsie brought out their Bible. The word of God gave light and hope in the darkness. 'Nothing can separate us from the love of God,' they read. Not even Ravensbruck.

At first Corrie and Betsie worked in a nearby factory. They had to push a heavy cart from a rail track to the factory gates. Back and forth they went, for eleven hours each day. They had a brief break at midday for a bowl of watery soup and a boiled potato. When they returned to the barracks the women were totally exhausted.

Twelve weeks after arriving they were moved to another block. It was an enormous room. 1400 women from Germany, Poland, France, Belgium and Austria, as well as Holland, were packed inside together.

Fleas!

Betsie and Corrie had to share a straw-covered platform with seven others. Corrie lay down, but shot up straightaway – something had bitten her.

'Fleas!' she cried. 'The place is crawling with them.'

Each night Corrie and Betsie brought out the Bible, and a crowd would gather round. They translated verses from Dutch

into German, then other women translated into Polish, French, Russian and Czech. So many wanted to join in that a second meeting was organised after evening roll-call.

Not once did a guard enter the room. They always kept away. It was hard to understand why, until one day Betsie overheard two guards talking. 'I'm not going in there,' one said to the other. 'It's crawling with fleas.' So Corrie and Betsie thanked God for fleas!

Another amazing thing happened. Night after night Corrie handed out a couple of vitamin drops to everyone who needed them: ten, twenty, sometimes thirty people. But the bottle of vitamin drops never dried up! It reminded Corrie of the Bible story where a poor widow's jar of oil lasted right through a famine.

One day a hospital worker managed to smuggle in a bag full of vitamin tablets. That very night, when Corrie tipped up the vitamin bottle, not a single drop appeared. It was empty!

Without explanation, the women were taken off factory work and told to shovel sand. Betsie was so weak she could hardly lift her shovel. She began to cough up blood. As her body grew weaker and weaker, she talked more and more to others about Jesus.

'Some of these people are so close to heaven!' she told Corrie.

A few days later Betsie herself died.

At first Corrie was scared to look at her sister's body. But when she did, she saw her face was radiant and peaceful. No more pain. No more suffering. Betsie was alive and well with Jesus in heaven. For the next few days the picture of Betsie's face helped Corrie to tell many women about the joy of heaven.

Shortly afterwards, one morning at roll-call, Corrie's name boomed out over the loudspeaker. She stepped forward. *What's going on?* she thought. *Am I in trouble? Has someone reported my Bible?*

Released!
A guard led her to an office, where she joined a line of prisoners.

'*Entlassen,*' (Dutch for 'released') said the man behind the desk.

'*Entlassen?* Released? Am I free?' Corrie puzzled.

She was handed a document with her name and date of birth on. 'CERTIFICATE OF DISCHARGE' was stamped across the top. For the next six days Corrie stayed in the camp hospital, waiting until she was fit enough to leave. While she was there, she cared for those who were too sick to move.

When the doctor said she could leave, Corrie could hardly believe it. A guard handed her some new, warm clothing and shoes, and returned her money, gold ring and watch. Full of fresh hope, Corrie found a Dutch girl in the ward to give her Bible to. 'Back in Holland I'll be able to get another,' she said.

The heavy iron doors of the camp swung open. Corrie hobbled out behind her woman guard. At the small railway station she was left on her own.

Can this be real? she wondered.

Three days later she was back in Holland. Hungry and weary, she found herself in the town of Groningen, on the Dutch border. The trains could go no further, because bombs had destroyed the tracks.

Corrie walked painfully to a Christian hospital near the station. For the first time in months she was lovingly cared for. Kind nurses brought her food and drink. She soaked in warm, soapy water, and dried herself on thick, fluffy towels. She slept in clean, white sheets with smooth, soft blankets and plump pillows. How different from Ravensbruck!

Home

After ten days some lorry drivers from her home town, Haarlem, arrived in Groningen, and the hospital arranged for Corrie to travel back with them.

Back home, Corrie discovered that she had been set free by mistake. A week after her release, all the women of her age in the camp were killed. Wandering through the deserted house, Corrie prayed, 'Thank you, Jesus, that I am alive. Now I am free, please show me what you want me to do.'

Corrie remembered how, in prison, God had given Betsie a vision of a beautiful home, where people who had been damaged by the war could be looked after. God had also told her that, after the war, they were to use a German prison camp to help the homeless. As well as this work, Corrie was to travel all over the world, telling people how God had been with them in Ravensbruck; how he had been their hiding place.

But now Betsie was dead. Corrie missed her so much. Then she thought of Betsie's words, 'We must tell people, Corrie. We know that the light of Jesus is stronger than the deepest darkness.'

When the war ended, a few months later, Corrie began

speaking in public all over Holland. In churches, club rooms and homes she talked about Ravensbruck, and about Betsie's vision to care for victims of the war.

With the help of a wealthy widow, Corrie set up the home she and Betsie had talked about. It was a fifty-six-room mansion, surrounded by vast gardens. News of the home spread, and soon it was full of former prisoners. Some had been in prison camps, others hidden away in attics and cupboards for two, three or four years.

Doctors, counsellors and health visitors gave their time, free of charge. People gave money, clothing and furniture. The war had only been over a few months when the director of an aid organisation offered Corrie another place to open a home.

'We've been given a prison camp in Germany,' he explained.

And so God's promise to Betsie became a reality. Soon the barbed-wire fences were replaced by flowers and plants. The drab, grey walls were painted a bright, cheerful green. Where once there had been cruelty and ugliness, now there was care and beauty.

Corrie travelled all over the world, telling people about these homes and about the love of God. Over a period of thirty-three years, she visited more than sixty countries, including Israel, Japan, Argentina, Britain, Vietnam, South Africa and Germany. Her message was simple but powerful: 'God's love is stronger than evil and death.'

Forgiven!

After one particular meeting, a guard who had worked in Ravensbruck came up to Corrie.

'I know God has forgiven me the cruel things I did there,' he said. 'I would like to hear you say that you forgive me too.' He held out his hand.

'Jesus, help me to forgive this man,' Corrie prayed. 'I can't do it on my own, but I know I must forgive those who have hurt me.'

As she prayed, a force shot down her arm and brought a feeling of true warmth and forgiveness. For a long moment they held hands.

'I forgive you, brother, with all my heart,' said Corrie, with tears in her eyes.

It was one of the most difficult things God had ever asked Corrie to do; but he gave her the power to do it.

Corrie also wrote many books, and helped to make a film called 'The Hiding Place', about her life in prison.

Corrie ten Boom died on her ninety-first birthday, leaving behind little money and few possessions. But the world is richer for her story of hope, love and courage.